THE OMEGA MUTAN

TRIAGE
CHRISTOPHER MUSE

TEMPUS
EVA BELL

MAGNETO
K LEHNSHERR

MAGIK
ILLYANA RASPUTIN

FABIO MEDIA

BENJAMIN DEEDS

BRIAN MICHAEL
BENDIS
WRITER

CHRIS
BACHALO
PENCILER, #27 & #29-31

KRIS
ANKA
ART/COLORS, #26 & #28

MARC
DEERING

WAYNE
FAUCHER

MARK
IRWIN

JAIME
MENDOZA

VICTOR
OLAZABA

TIM
TOWNSEND

AL
VEY

INKERS, #27 & #29-31

CHRIS
BACHALO

RAIN
BEREDO

ANTONIO
FABELA

JOSE
VILLARRUBIA

COLORISTS, #27 & #29-31

COVER ART: **CHRIS BACHALO & TIM TOWNSEND** (#26-27, #29, #31) AND **KRIS ANKA** (#28, #30)
LETTERER: **VC'S JOE CARAMAGNA**   ASSISTANT EDITOR: **XANDER JAROWEY**   EDITOR: **MIKE MARTS**

X-MEN CREATED BY **STAN LEE & JACK KIRBY**

COLLECTION EDITOR: **JENNIFER GRÜNWALD** ASSOCIATE MANAGING EDITOR: **ALEX STARBUCK**
EDITOR, SPECIAL PROJECTS: **MARK D. BEAZLEY** SENIOR EDITOR, SPECIAL PROJECTS: **JEFF YOUNGQUIST**
SVP PRINT, SALES & MARKETING: **DAVID GABRIEL** BOOK DESIGNER: **RODOLFO MURAGUCHI**

EDITOR IN CHIEF: **AXEL ALONSO** CHIEF CREATIVE OFFICER: **JOE QUESADA**
PUBLISHER: **DAN BUCKLEY** EXECUTIVE PRODUCER: **ALAN FINE**

Born with genetic mutations that gave them abilities beyond those of normal humans, mutants are the next stage in evolution. As such, they are feared and hated by humanity. A group of mutants known as the X-Men fight for peaceful coexistence between mutants and humankind. But not all mutants see peaceful coexistence as a reality.

Cyclops is the public face of what he calls "the new mutant revolution." Vowing to protect the mutant race, he's begun to gather and train a new generation of young mutants.

Recently, She-Hulk arrived at the Jean Grey School for higher learning with a startling pacakage for the X-Men, the last will and testament of Charles Xavier! Appearing as a hologram, Xavier revealed that at the time of his death, he was married to Raven Darkholme, A.K.A. Mystique. When he first developed Cerebro, Xavier discovered a mutant, Matthew Malloy, whose abilities were so great and terrifying that he was forced to erase the young man's memory of his powers. With his death, the mental blocks that Xavier had been keeping in place have been weakening, leaving the X-Men with the task of finding and securing Matthew before the threat he poses becomes real. Little do they know that Matthew's re-emerging powers have already brought him to the attention of S.H.I.E.L.D.!

THIS IS IT.

MATTHEW MALLOY
AMERICAN CITIZEN
COLLEGE EDUCATION: NORTHWESTERN UNIVERSITY
NO PRIOR ARRESTS
OMEGA LEVEL POWER INDICATED
NEWBERRY, SOUTH CAROLINA CASUALTY ESTIMATE INCOMPLETE

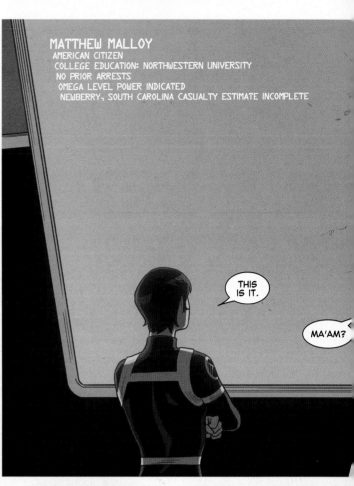

THIS IS IT.

MA'AM?

S.H.I.E.L.D. HELICARRIER.
FLOATING 1,000 FEET SOUTH OF NEWBERRY, SOUTH CAROLINA.

I THOUGHT TO MYSELF--THAT IS *MY* NIGHTMARE, TOO.

AND--AND THIS IS IT.

THIS IS THE NIGHTMARE. THIS IS OUR NIGHTMARE.

GET THE AVENGERS NOW.

THEY ARE OFF PLANET, COMMANDER HILL.

ALL OF THEM? THERE'S FIFTY TEAMS.

THE ONES WE NEED FOR THIS? THEY ARE OFF PLANET, MA'AM.

WHAT ABOUT THE FANTASTIC FOUR?

DON'T ASK.

LAST YEAR, I OVERHEARD TONY STARK AND NICK FURY TALKING.

THIS WAS AFTER A MAJOR ATTACK BY, WELL, IT'S CLASSIFIED.

TONY STARK SAID HE HAD FIVE NIGHTMARES.

FIVE NIGHTMARE SCENARIOS THAT KEPT HIM UP AT NIGHT.

BEFORE HE COULD EVER SAY WHAT THEY WERE FURY SNARLED BACK AT HIM-- I ONLY GOT *ONE* NIGHTMARE.

MY NIGHTMARE IS THAT SOME GUY, JUST SOME GUY, WAKES UP ONE MORNING WITH THE POWER OF *GOD*.

HE DOESN'T KNOW HOW HE GOT IT, HE DOESN'T KNOW WHAT TO DO WITH IT, AND HE JUST $#%&$#% HICCUPS AND THOUSANDS OF PEOPLE $#%&$#% DIE.

EVACUATE THE ENTIRE STATE OF SOUTH CAROLINA!

MA'AM?

YOU HEARD ME.

THERE IS AN MEGA THREAT PROTOCOL!

FIRST STEP IS EVACUATION!

QUICKLY AND QUIETLY EMPTY THE ENTIRE STATE.

I DON'T CARE WHERE THEY GO OR WHERE YOU PUT THEM...

...NOBODY ELSE DIES TODAY.

"NO!"

THE JEAN GREY SCHOOL.

I SAID *NO!*

NO, TO WHAT PART, SCOTT?

I'M NOT DOING IT.

I'M OUT.

YOU WANNA BET THERE, SLIM?

HE *LIED* TO US. XAVIER LIED TO *ALL* OF US.

ALL OUR $#%#$%& ASIDE, LOGAN. HE LIED TO US.

HE TOLD US TO ACT ONE WAY AS X-MEN AND BEHIND OUR BACKS HE ACTED ANOTHER.

WE ALWAYS TEASED HIM THAT HIS PSYCHIC POWERS LET HIM DO PRETTY MUCH WHATEVER HE WANTED. BUT HE CONVINCED US OF THIS HIGHER STANDARD.

OUR #$%#$%% NOT ASIDE.

CHARLES XAVIER HAD A DYING WISH AND WE ARE GOING TO *FULFILL* THAT DYING WISH.

NO.

GET ON THE PLANE.

CHARLES XAVIER'S LAST WISH WAS FOR YOU AND LOGAN AND RACHEL TO GO AND TAKE CARE OF SOMETHING.

SO TAKE CARE OF IT.

ACTUALLY HIS LAST WISH WAS PROBABLY LIKE--SCOTT SUMMERS, I WISH YOU WEREN'T KILLING ME RIGHT NOW.

SO CUT THE TRADEMARK SCOTT SUMMERS HOLIER-THAN-THOU HYPOCRITE SONG AND DANCE AND GET ON THE PLANE.

HE WOULD HAVE DONE IT FOR YOU.

NOTHING ELSE MATTERS.

YOU SURE YOU DON'T WANT MORE OF US TO COME?

IF WE NEED MORE, WE'LL CALL.

I'M VERY CONFIDENT RACHEL CAN HANDLE THIS.

THAT MAKES *ONE* OF US.

YOU WERE NOT EXAGGERATING ABOUT OUR DEAR MR. SUMMERS.

THAT IS UPSETTING.

I FEEL BAD FOR HIM.

YOU DO?

HE'S SUFFERING.

HE'S IN--HE'S CLEARLY STILL IN SHOCK OVER XAVIER'S DEATH.

LOOK AT HIM.

HE KILLED CHARLES XAVIER-- HIS FATHER FIGURE.

IT WAS AN ACCIDENT, IT WASN'T HIS FAULT, BUT STILL...IT HAPPENED.

BOBBY, YOU CAN EMPATHIZE WITH HIM AND STILL--

CHARLES XAVIER IS DEAD!

HOW ABOUT WE DON'T DO WHAT WE ALWAYS DO. WE *DON'T* JUST PRETEND THE BAD THINGS DIDN'T HAPPEN.

SCOTT SUMMERS RUINED US.

THIS SCHOOL WILL NEVER BE THE SAME. *WE* WILL NEVER BE THE SAME.

AND IT JUST MIGHT BE THAT EVERYTHING HAPPENS FOR A REASON...AND THAT WHAT COMES NEXT WILL BE AMONG OUR FINEST--

STOP!

STOP.

YOU THINK SCOTT SUMMERS IS IN SHOCK?

I THINK *I* WAS IN SHOCK AND I JUST COMIN' OUT OF IT.

WHAT WOULD YOU HAVE US DO?

HONESTLY, I KIND OF HOPE HE DIES IN BATTLE...

...PUT HIM OUT OF OUR MISERY.

I KNOW THAT'S WRONG, BUT IT'S HONEST.

AND IF THAT DOESN'T HAPPEN?

NOTHING WE DO, NOTHING HE DOES, IS GOING TO MAKE THAT NOT HAVE HAPPENED.

"DON'T YOU THINK WHEN HE CLOSES HIS EYES AT NIGHT THE FIRST THING HE SEES IS CHARLES XAVIER'S DEAD BODY LYING ON THE GROUND IN FRONT OF HIM?

"IT'S OKAY TO BE MAD AT HIM IF THAT'S HOW YOU GUYS DEAL WITH ALL THIS...BUT THAT MAN IS SUFFERING."

DON'T YOU THINK HE--

PLEASE, ANGELICA, DON'T!

DON'T MAKE ME SYMPATHIZE WITH SCOTT SUMMERS' PLIGHT.

DON'T MAKE ME FEEL BAD FOR HIM!

MAYBE IT'S LOOKING AT XAVIER'S HOLOGRAM TODAY OR HEARING THIS CRAZINESS THAT HE MARRIED MYSTIQUE.

BUT I'M ANGRY!

I'M REALLY, REALLY ANGRY THAT SCOTT SUMMERS MURDERED THE MAN WHO GAVE ME THIS LIFE!

GAVE MY ENTIRE LIFE PURPOSE!

I'M ANGRY!

AND I'M GETTING ANGRIER BY THE SECOND!

HOW AM I DOING THIS?

OKAY, OKAY... ...THIS IS TOO CREEPY.

COMMANDER HILL, S.H.I.E.L.D.'S PSI DIVISION IS HERE.

COMMANDER, I AM *BENNET DU PARIS.* MY PRESENCE HAS BEEN REQUESTED.

THIS IS *HEADLOK.* HE IS ON LOAN FROM--

YOU SOUNDED LIKE YOU NEEDED THE BEST PSYCHICS I COULD GET MY HANDS ON.

NO TIME FOR CHIT-CHAT.

I NEED YOU TO REACH INSIDE THAT MAN AND SHUT HIM DOWN.

TO MAKE HIM SLEEP OR--

WHATEVER YOU HAVE TO DO.

THE PROBLEM IS I CAN'T GET YOU ANY CLOSER, PHYSICALLY, THAN THIS.

THE TWO OF US WILL CREATE A MIND CONNECTION.

BASICALLY, HE'LL ANCHOR ME WHILE I ENTER THE MAN'S HEAD.

FROM HERE.

DO IT.

NOW.

HIS NAME IS MATTHEW.

HE IS A BORN MUTANT.

CHARLES XAVIER?

DON'T.

ALL AGENTS! CLEAR THE WAR ROOM! WE ARE UNDER ATTACK!

GEEZ.

HE *IS* A MUTANT.

THUD

$#%&!

GET ME THE X-MEN.

POINK! POINK!

POINK! POINK!

TOO LATE!

GOLDBALLS!

OH, GOOD LORD! NOW IT'S YOUR CATCHPHRASE?!

GOLDBALLS!

OUR HIVE MIND DOESN'T WORK. IRON MAN'S ARMOR IS BLOCKING US.

YEAH, HOW ABOUT THAT?

I MEAN, I'M NOT FIGHTING THE AVENGERS BECAUSE IT, BY DEFINITION, MAKES US THE--

AAOOWW!

REVOLUTIONARIES.

NO... I MEAN... IF THEY'RE THE GOOD GUYS...

...DOESN'T THAT BY DEFINITION MAKE US THE *BAD GUYS?*

I DON'T AGREE WITH ANY OF THOSE SIMPLISTIC LABELS.

WELL, MOST OF THE WORLD *DOES.*

"MOST OF THE WORLD." MOST OF THE WORLD EATS PROCESSED FOODS. MOST OF THE WORLD IS GLEEFULLY STUPID.

SO YOU'RE OKAY WITH THIS? US TRAINING TO SPECIFICALLY TAKE ON THE AVENGERS? TO TAKE ON AUTHORITY?

CHRIS...WE'VE, MY SISTERS AND I, HAVE BEEN AT THIS A LITTLE LONGER THAN YOU...

...WE'VE BEEN *MUTANTS* A LITTLE LONGER THAN YOU.

WE'RE TRAINING TO FIGHT FOR OUR RIGHTS AS MUTANTS.

"WHETHER YOU SEE OR NOT, WHETHER YOU AGREE WITH IT OR NOT...

...WE, MUTANTS, US, WE'RE A THREAT TO THE HOMO SAPIEN ESTABLISHMENT.

WE'RE TRAINING TO FIGHT BACK.

NO. WE'RE TRAINING FOR THE COMING "MUTANT REVOLUTION."

THAT, TOO.

AND WHAT FORM WILL THAT TAKE?

WELL, IF IT TAKES THE FORM OF THE AVENGERS KNOCKING DOWN OUR FRONT DOOR...I'D LIKE TO BE READY.

WE HAVEN'T HAD A MOMENT TO TALK ABOUT ANY OF THIS.

IT'S BEEN BEDLAM SINCE WE JOINED THIS THING...

...NOBODY ELSE FINDS THIS INCREASINGLY SQUIRRELLY?

I'M ALONE HERE?

MAYBE WE SHOULD WAIT TILL THE ADULTS GET BACK AND TALK ABOUT IT THEN.

ADULTS? I'M THIRTY YEARS OLD.

YOU KNOW WHAT I MEAN.

WELL...WHAT AN AWKWARD SILENCE FOR EVERYONE BUT THE PSYCHIC SISTERS.

GUESS I STRUCK A NERVE.

HEY, McCOY, YOU HAVE ANY IDEA WHERE WE'RE GOING?

I AM IN CEREBRO NOW...TRYING TO LOCK DOWN COORDINATES.

XAVIER HAD HIDDEN THIS MUTANT FROM ME, FROM US, FOR YEARS, SO TRYING TO PINPOINT HIS EXACT LOCATION IS A BIT OF A CHALLENGE.

THIS MAN IS ON THE GRID. I HAVE HIS NORMAL, AVERAGE *HOMO SAPIEN* LIFE RIGHT HERE.

WE KNOW WHERE THIS MATTHEW MALLOY LIVES, BUT WE DON'T KNOW IF-- HOLD ON...

I THINK I HAVE SOMETHING.

I THINK I FOUND IT, HOLD ON...

OH, MY STARS AND...

HOLD ON THERE, FUZZBALL, SOMETHING AIN'T RIGHT.

SOMETHING JUST--

--CAME OUT OF NO--

X-MEN, THIS IS MARIA HILL.

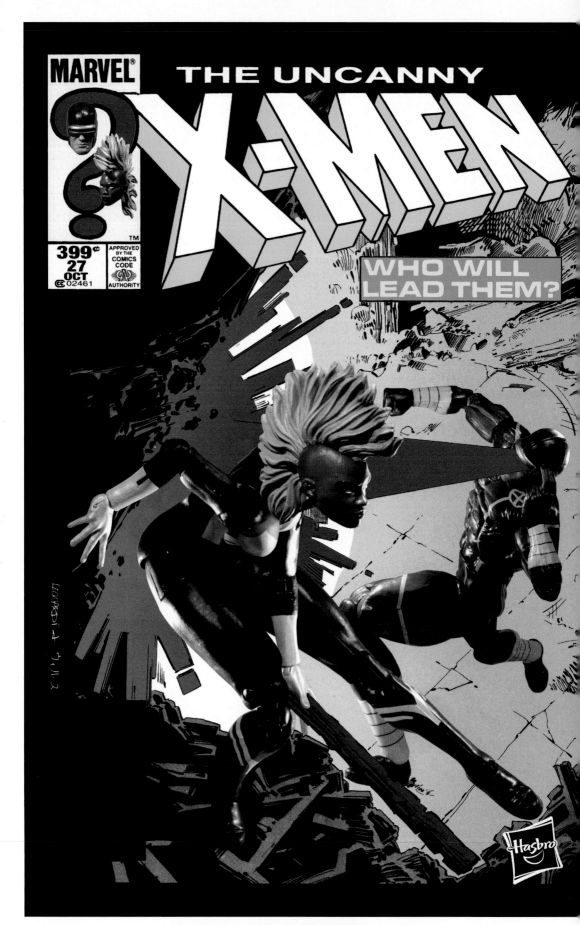

UNCANNY X-MEN #27 HASBRO VARIANT

YOU NEED NOT BLAME YOURSELF, MATTHEW.

THIS POWER IS NOT SOMETHING ANY ONE MAN COULD CONTROL.

CAN--CAN WE FIX THIS? CAN WE MAKE THIS RIGHT?

I PROMISE WE WILL TRY.

IF YOU LET ME.

WAIT...

...WHY ARE WE TRYING TO STOP ME FROM BEING WHAT I'M SUPPOSED TO BE?

BECAUSE PEOPLE'S LIVES ARE IN DANGER.

YOUR LIFE IS IN DANGER.

UH-OH.

MAYBE I AM SUPPOSED TO BE ABLE TO DO THESE THINGS.

MAYBE IT'S A MORTAL SIN TO STAND IN THE WAY OF THIS POWER.

MATTHEW...

I HAVE A POWER GREATER THAN ANY OF YOU.

MAYBE I'M SUPPOSED TO HAVE IT.

MAYBE I'M THIS WAY FOR A REASON AND MAYBE YOU WERE WRONG FOR STANDING IN MY WAY.

MATTHEW, YOU NEED TO CALM DOWN...

WHY HAVE YOU BEEN TRYING TO STOP ME FROM BEING MYSELF ALL THESE YEARS?

YOU KNOW THAT'S NOT--

WHO ARE YOU?

MATTHEW--

YOU ARE NOT CHARLES XAVIER.

MATTHEW, PLEASE!

GET OUT OF THERE!

ALL STATIONS! PULL THIS BOAT BACK BEFORE--

THIS RIGHT HERE, YOU...THIS IS ALL IN MY HEAD, ISN'T IT?

YOU REALLY SHOULDN'T BE IN MY HEAD.

WE'RE JUST TRYING TO HELP YOU--

OH NO.

CHARLES XAVIER IS DEAD.

UH-OH.

ORORO?!
ORORO!

SHE'S BLEEDING.

I CAN WAKE HER UP TELEPATHICALLY.

ORORO!

nngddss

OH, THANK GOD!

HOW LONG...HAVE I BEEN OUT?

BELIEVE IT OR NOT, ABOUT TWO MINUTES.

WHAT?

HOW DID I END UP IN MY ROOM?

THE NEW MUTANT.

HE--HE PUT YOU HERE. HE SENT US HOME.

HE DESTROYED A HELICARRIER AND SENT YOU TWO HOME?

WHERE'S WOLVERINE? WHERE'S SCOTT?

THEY'RE NOT HERE. MAYBE HE ONLY SPARED US.

THIS MUTANT DESTROYED AN ENTIRE HELICARRIER?!

WITH A WAVE OF HIS HAND.

AND IT'S MY FAULT.

I--I ENGAGED HIM TOO HARD.

I PUSHED. IT WAS TOO--

RACHEL, YOU WERE SENT THERE TO ENGAGE HIM.

BY CHARLES XAVIER HIMSELF.

HE WAS TOO POWERFUL, MAGIK.

I FAILED.

AND HE SPARED YOU TWO?

FASCINATING.

JUST EXPERIENCED SOMETHING I HAVE NEVER EXPERIENCED BEFORE.

AND YOU'VE BEEN AROUND.

YEAH. XAVIER WAS RIGHT.

THIS MUTANT IS-- IS--I'VE NEVER--

I'LL TAKE YOU BACK TO THE JEAN GREY SCHOOL.

THE X-MEN ARE GATHERING FROM ALL CORNERS AND BEAST IS REACHING OUT TO THE MUTANT-FRIENDLY WORLD GOVERNMENTS, THE AVENGERS, FANTASTIC FOUR...AND HE'S TRYING TO COME UP WITH A PLAN B.

OKAY.

NO...

NO.

WAIT.

NO TO WHICH PART?

YOU ARE NOT THINKING WHAT WE SEE YOU'RE THINKING...

THAT'S--

THAT'S-- WOW.

THAT IS A CRAZY PLAN, PROFESSOR SUMMERS.

UNCANNY X-MEN #27 DEADPOOL 75TH ANNIVERSARY VARIANT
BY MIKE MCKONE & JASON KEITH

NEWBERRY, SOUTH CAROLINA.

SCOTT SUMMERS!

NO!

OH, GOD.

THEY HATE ME.

THEY HATE WHAT THEY DON'T UNDERSTAND.

BREATHE DEEP, MATTHEW.

WE ARE ABOUT TO TELEPORT. IT IS A SENSATION.

UM, WHERE ARE WE GOING?

YOU WANT TO TRUST THIS LADY WHEN IT COMES TO THIS.

DEEP BREATH.

I PROMISE THIS DOESN'T HURT.

NOT EVEN A BIT.

OKAY.

WE'RE DOING IT TOGETHER.

WHAT SHOULD WE DO, COMMANDER HILL?

THE MUTANT THAT DECLA A REVOLUTION AGAINST JUST WALKED OFF WITH MOST POWERFUL MUTA IN THE WORLD.

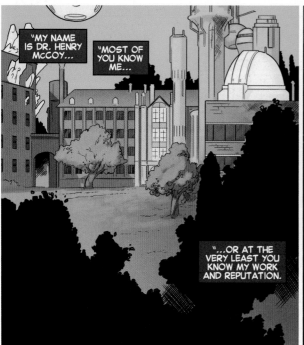

"MY NAME IS DR. HENRY McCOY...

"MOST OF YOU KNOW ME...

"...OR AT THE VERY LEAST YOU KNOW MY WORK AND REPUTATION.

"THE X-MEN HAVE A SERIOUS AND IMMEDIATE SITUATION AND WE NEED YOUR HELP.

"WE HAVE DISCOVERED A ARE IN PURSUIT AN OMEGA-LEV NEW MUTANT

"WE HAVE TO WORK TOGETHER TO QUICKLY FIND A WAY TO EITHER TEMPER THE MUTANT'S POWER LEVEL, SEND IT SOMEWHERE WHERE IT CANNOT HURT ANY OTHER LIVING CREATURE, OR *DESTROY* IT.

"BUT WHAT WE CANNOT DO IS ALLOW THIS MUTANT OUT IN THE OPEN FOR ONE SECOND LONGER.

"BE ADVISED-- ATTACKING THIS MUTANT HEAD ON IS A FATAL ERROR.

"WHAT WE M DO IS STUDY OVERALL--

HENRY?

AND THEY ARE CHOOSING NOT TO RESPOND.

NOT ONE GOVERNMENT.

NOT THE UNITED NATIONS.

NO ONE WILL HELP US.

THESE SHORTSIGHTED HUMANS CARE MORE ABOUT DISTANCING THEMSELVES FROM US THAN WORKING TOGETHER TO SOLVE THIS PROBLEM THAT AFFECTS US ALL!

YOU CAN EXAMINE ME LATER, HENRY.

WE NEED TO FIND SCOTT SUMMERS...AND NEED TO FIND HIM RIGHT NOW.

CAN YOU SEE SCOTT SUMMERS WITH CEREBRO?

WHY?

WHAT HAPPENED?

WHAT DID HE DO NOW?

HE TOOK THE NEW MUTANT.

HE TOOK HIM?

WE RECEIVED THIS INFORMATION DIRECTLY FROM S.H.I.E.L.D.

THE MUTANT CRASHED A HELICARRIER, FOR SOME REASON SPARED ALL OF THE X-MEN...

...AND THEN SCOTT SUMMERS SCOOPED HIM UP WHILE EVERYONE ELSE WAS RUNNING AROUND IN A PANIC.

PRETTY MUCH.

"...YOU AND I HAVE A LOT IN COMMON.

"I, TOO, WAS BORN WITH A DESTRUCTIVE POWER I DID NOT UNDERSTAND AND COULD NOT CONTROL.

"AT A VERY YOUNG AGE I WAS SURE THAT MY LIFE HAD BEEN RUINED, THAT I WOULD NEVER HAVE HAPPINESS, AND THAT MY BIRTHRIGHT WAS A CURSE.

"AND I WAS AN ORPHAN.

"THERE WAS NO ONE TO HELP ME.

"NO ONE TO HELP ME UNDERSTAND HOW THE WORLD WORKED OR WHAT WAS HAPPENING TO ME.

"UNTIL CHARLES XAVIER FOUND ME.

I DON'T KNOW WHAT I WOULD HAVE DONE IF HE HAD NOT COME ALONG.

"I CAN HONESTLY SAY HE SAVED MY LIFE.

"HE SAVED IT AND HE GAVE IT PURPOSE.

"AND THEN..."

WE RISE UP.

TAKE OUR PLACE.

WE ASKED FOR OUR PLACE, WE BEGGED FOR IT, WE FOUGHT FOR IT, WE SUFFERED FOR IT...BUT THEY REFUSE TO GIVE IT TO US.

WE HAVE TO TAKE IT BECAUSE NOTHING ELSE WORKS.

AND DO WHAT?

...U HAVE ...ONTROL ...URSELF ...NOW.

YOU NEED TO BE ABLE TO TALK ABOUT THINGS WITHOUT RIPPING THE ENVIRONMENT AROUND YOU APART WHEN A BAD THOUGHT ENTERS YOUR HEAD.

I-I CAN'T.

YOU CAN!

YOU HAVE TO!

YOU CAN CONTROL YOUR BREATHING, YOUR HEART, YOU CONTROL EVERY PART OF YOURSELF!

NO. I K-K-KILLED ALL THOSE PEOPLE!

MY HEART BREAKS FOR EVERY SINGLE LIFE YOU ACCIDENTALLY TOOK!

BUT I CAN *HELP* YOU WITH THAT!

NO ONE CAN HELP ME!

WHERE WE'RE GOING... YOU WILL SAVE FIFTY TIMES AS MANY LIVES!

AT LEAST!

YOU AND I--WE ARE GOING TO BALANCE YOUR KARMIC DEBT!

I AM GOING TO HELP YOU DO IT!

I'M GOING TO SAVE LIVES AS PART OF YOUR REVOLUTION?!

ABSOLUTELY.

YOU MIGHT SAVE AN ENTIRE SPECIES.

NO! NO! YOU'RE GOING TO USE ME TO SCARE THEM!

THEY'RE GOING TO BE SCARED OF YOU NO MATTER WHAT I DO.

RRRR!

MATTHEW.

LOOK INTO MY MIND.

YOU'RE NOT THE FIRST MUTANT TO BE IN THIS POSITION!

YOU'RE NOT THE FIRST!

"YOU'RE NOT THE FIRST MUTANT TO BE IN THIS POSITION.

"YOU'RE NOT THE FIRST ONE OF US TO BE TESTED AND CHALLENGED BY THE VERY NATURE OF YOUR POWER.

"THERE HAVE BEEN MANY OF US HOLDING POWER THAT CONSUMES US...THAT CONSUMES EVERYTHING AROUND US.

"AND MORE TIMES THAN NOT THOSE POOR SOULS WERE DESTROYED FROM INSIDE AND OUT.

"EACH AND EVERY ONE A CAUTIONARY TALE.

"THAT DOESN'T HAVE TO HAPPEN TO YOU.

"EVERY SINGLE TRAGEDY THAT HAS BEFALLEN OUR PEOPLE HAS BEEN SOMETHING THAT COULD'VE BEEN AVOIDED.

"WE CAN LEARN FROM OUR MISTAKES.

"WE *HAVE* TO.

"I'M TELLING YOU...YOU CAN BEAT THIS.

"I'M TELLING YOU...YOU CAN BE ONE OF THE GREATS.

"DON'T REPEAT THE SAME MISTAKES I HAVE MADE.

"DON'T LET THE POWER *CONSUME* YOU."

AND I THINK IT'S TIME TO GET EMMA.

NOT YET.

PUT ME BACK UP THERE.

NO.

IN THIS SECRET SORCERESS TRAINING THAT YOU'RE WORKING ON IN YOUR SPARE TIME...

...HAVE YOU LEARNED ANYTHING THAT COULD HELP US WITH THIS?

YOU'RE TRYING TO GET RID OF ME.

AFTER ALL WE'VE BEEN THROUGH YOU NEED TO TRUST ME.

PUT ME BACK UP THERE AND GO FIND A WAY TO HEAL OUR NEW BROTHER.

YOU KEEP USING THE WORD "BROTHER."

IT REMINDS ME OF THE WORD "BROTHERHOOD."

ILLYANA.

ONE MORE CHANCE.

BUT AFTER THAT...

...IF I COME BACK AND DON'T LIKE WHAT I SEE, IT WON'T BE YOUR CALL ANYMORE.

I BELIEVE WILL REGRET THIS.

HEY... WHAT HAPPENED TO THE BREAKFAST?

I'M NOT A WAITRESS.

I THOUGHT YOU WERE GETTING THOSE $30 PANCAKES FROM NEW ORLEANS THAT WE LOVE.

YOU'RE HUNGRY?

SCOTT...

...WHAT IF CHARLES XAVIER WAS RIGHT ABOUT MATTHEW?

UNCANNY X-MEN #27 VARIANT
BY MICO SUAYAN & EDGAR DELGADO

29

YEARS AGO...

DR. STRANGE, I--?

OH. YOU'RE NOT HERE.

I'M ASSUMING THIS IS *WORTH* BREAKING ALL THE TIME-SPACE CONTINUUM PROTOCOLS TO COME HERE.

THERE IS A MUTANT WHO HAS REVEALED ITSELF TO HAVE AN UNCONTROLLABLE, *ABOVE* OMEGA-LEVEL POWER.

YOU'RE NOT SUPPOSED TO TELL ME OF MY FUTURE.

I'M TELLING YOU AS LITTLE AS I CAN.

WHAT IS *OMEGA-LEVEL?* WHAT DOES THAT MEAN?

THIS PARTICULAR MUTANT HAS POWER OVER TIME AND SPACE AND LIFE-AND-DEATH AND HAS NO ABILITY TO *CONTROL* IT.

OKAY.

THAT *WAS* WORTH COMING HERE.

DID YOU GO TO MY FUTURE SELF FIRST?

NO.

AND I SHOULDN'T ASK *WHY?*

NO.

AND YOU WANT TO DO WHAT?

YOU WANT TO FIX THIS MUTANT?

PUT THIS MUTANT DOWN?

SOMEONE I SOMETIM[ES] ADMIRE WANT[S TO] TRY AND SAVE [OR] SALVAGE TH[E] MUTANT.

IS THERE IN THE BO[OK] OF VISHANTI, ANY OF THE SCROLLS.

...IS THERE A SPELL OR A SERIES OF SPELLS THAT I CAN APPLY TO THE SITUATION THAT ALLOWS THIS MUTANT TO LIVE A NORMAL AND PRODUCTIVE LIFE WITHOUT TAKING AWAY HIS BIRTHRIGHT BUT WITHOUT RISKING EVERYONE ELSE'S LIFE?

I WISH YOU WOULD TELL ME HOW FAR IN THE FUTURE YOU'RE FROM.

WE BOTH KNOW THAT'S NOT A GOOD IDEA.

DO WE?

YOU COME IN HERE IN A HARRIED HURRY... ABOUT AN UNCONTROLLABLE MUTANT WHO IS ABOUT TO WHAT?

RIP THE EARTH IN HALF?

IN THE FUTURE I MIGHT ONLY HAVE SO MUCH TIME LEFT ON THIS PLANET.

THAT IS LIFE.

I GUESS IT IS.

WHAT ABOUT A VISHANTI GUSANI SPELL CYCLE?

NO. THAT IS NOT A GOOD IDEA EVEN IN THE *BEST* OF CIRCUMSTANCES.

A CYTTORAK FIRE DANCE?

NOT UNLESS YOU WANT A DOORWAY FROM THE DARK DIMENSION TO OPEN UP IN FRONT OF YOU...

CONJURING THE MISTS OF IKTHALON?

WE COULDN'T FIND THAT MANY TURTLES.

OMEGA-LEVEL...

...HUH.

WHAT?

DEVIL'S TOWER, RIGHT NOW.

MAGNETO?

DON'T GET TOO EXCITED, MATTHEW.

I CAN TELL ALREADY THAT THIS IS HOLIER-THAN-THOU, HYPOCRITE MAGNETO ABOUT TO GIVE US AN EARFUL OF HOLIER-THAN-THOU HYPOCRISY.

GOODBYE.

NOOO!

DID-- DID YOU--

NO. NO, OF COURSE NOT.

HE IS ONE OF US.

I'VE NEVER BEEN PART OF AN "US" BEFORE.

I JUST DIDN'T WANT HIM HERE.

WHERE-- WHERE DID YOU SEND HIM?

SAME PLACE I SENT YOU WHEN WE FIRST MET...

WAIT!

WAIT FOR WHAT?

SHE COULD!

SHE COULD GO BACK IN TIME AND SAVE HIS LIFE!

IS-- IS THAT *BAD*?

IS IT BAD TO SAVE CHARLES XAVIER?

IS IT BAD TO SAVE *ANYONE*?

YOU-- YOU COULD GO FAR BACK IN TIME?

JUST LIKE THAT?

YOU'RE THAT GOOD AT IT NOW?

WELL, NO, IT TAKES SOME DOING.

DON'T TOUCH ME!

AND DON'T TELL ME WHAT I'VE LEARNED AND WHAT I'VE LOST!

WHEN-- *WHAT* DID YOU LOSE?

YEAH, DID SOMETHING HAPPEN THAT WE DON'T KNOW ABOUT?

SO YOU'VE LEARNED NOTHING?

EVERYTHING YOU'VE BEEN THROUGH?

EVERYTHING YOU'VE LOST?

AND YOU LEARNED NOTHING!

T WAS UST AN DEA. I THINK I CAN HELP HERE.

WHAT IF MAGNETO'S RIGHT?

WHAT IF PROFESSOR SUMMERS IS ABOUT TO MAKE A HUGE MISTAKE?

MAYBE I CAN STOP IT BEFORE IT HAPPENS!

IF MAGNETO IS RIGHT, I'LL MAKE US ALL T-SHIRTS THAT SAY, "MAGNETO IS--"

THEN WHERE'S THE LINE, EVA? YOU'RE PLAYING WITH, MAYBE, EVERYONE'S LIVES.

YEAH, THIS SOUNDS LIKE-- I DON'T KNOW, YOU MIGHT MAKE IT WORSE.

OR I MIGHT SAVE EVERYONE.

I MIGHT MAKE EVERYTHING BETTER.

YOU'VE LEARNED NOTHING.

THEY STUCK US HERE, EMMA.

I WAS JUST THINKING THAT.

NO WAY BACK TO OUR SCHOOL.

NO PLANE. NO TELEPORTER.

SHOULD WE CALL A CAB?

I THINK SOMETHING *BAD* HAS HAPPENED.

WELL, PROFESSOR KITTY, YOU ONLY THINK THAT BECAUSE YOU *ALWAYS* THINK THAT.

AND I'M ALWAYS *RIGHT*, EMMA.

TRUE.

WHAT SHOULD WE DO, SERIOUSLY?

MYSTIQUE ISN'T GOING TO COME HERE, ALISON.

IT'S NOT GOING TO HAPPEN.

I THOUGHT YOUR PSYCHIC POWERS WERE BROKEN, EMMA.

THEY ARE.

YOU'RE AN OPEN BOOK, DARLING.

ONE DAMAGED, OPEN BOOK.

AND, WOW, YOU SHOULD TALK, MS. FROST.

DON'T BE CATTY.

WE'RE ALL $#%&ED, WE'RE THE X-MEN.

YOU'RE STILL HERE.

GOOD.

WHAT HAPPENED *NOW*, BEAST?

I MADE A HUGE MISTAKE.

NO KIDDING?

EASY.

I REACHED OUT TO THE HUMAN AUTHORITIES AND AVENGERS ABOUT THIS NEW MUTANT SITUATION.

WHY?

BECAUSE IT IS BEYOND US AND I THOUGHT THEY WOULD HELP.

WHY?

A MOMENTARY FLASH OF HOPE FOR THE WORLD.

I TOLD YOU ABOUT HAVING THOSE.

ARE THE AVENGERS COMING?

NO.

ANYONE?

NOPE.

WELL, AIN'T THAT GREAT.

OH, HANK'S NOT DONE YET.

I WAS POKING AROUND SOME OF MY HACK WORK INTO THE GOVERNMENT AND AVENGERS SECURE SERVERS.

THEY ARE GOING TO *ATTACK*.

THEY MIGHT ALREADY BE DOING IT.

THEY'RE GOING TO ATTACK THE MUTANT THAT ALREADY CRASHED A HELICARRIER?

AND WHERE IS SCOTT SUMMERS IN ALL THIS?

"RIGHT WHERE HE SHOULDN'T BE."

MATTHEW?

I APPRECIATE WHAT YOU ARE DOING, SCOTT.

I DO.

I JUST-- I DON'T THINK I WAS MEANT TO BE HERE.

HERE?

ON THIS PLANET.

LIKE, YOU WANT TO LEAVE THE *PLANET?*

NO.

WHAT? NO.

I AM-- I AM CLEARLY A DANGER TO EVERYONE AND EVERYTHING.

CLEARLY.

XAVIER TRIED TO STOP IT, BUT ALL HE DID WAS DELAY IT.

I CAN HELP YOU.

YOU'LL NEVER HELP ME GET OVER THE FACT THAT PEOPLE HAVE DIED BECAUSE OF ME.

YOU'LL MAKE IT UP.

YOU'LL SAVE SO MANY.

I KNOW THAT'S WHAT YOU DO.

YOU CONVINCE YOURSELF THAT IT BALANCES OUT. BUT IT DOESN'T.

YOU KILL... YOU ARE A *KILLER.* THE END.

I KILLED.

I CAN KILL AGAIN. BY ACCIDENT.

IF I STUB MY TOE.

I--I JUST DON'T BELONG HERE.

YOU DON'T *KNOW* THAT.

NO, SCOTT.

YOU DON'T.

I DO.

I...I...

THERE'S A WAY TO FIND OUT.

UNCANNY X-MEN #29 75TH ANNIVERSARY VARIANT
BY ALEX ROSS

30

NEWBERRY, SOUTH CAROLINA.

DEVIL'S TOWER.

THIS IS MARIA HILL.

I WANT YOU TO *REPEAT* WHAT YOU JUST SAID.

THE NEW MUTANT, *MATTHEW MALLOY*, ALONG WITH *ILLYANA RASPUTIN* AND *SCOTT SUMMERS*, HAS BEEN STRUCK DOWN BY S.H.I.E.L.D. MISSILE FIRE.

ALL ORGANIC LIFE IN THE AREA HAS BEEN ELIMINATED.

THERE IS NOTHING HERE BUT DUST AND BONES.

SCOTT SUMMERS HAS BEEN ASSASSINATED.

I--I WANT FULL VISUAL CONFIRMATION AND IDENTIFICATION.

OH, MY GOD. WHAT HAPPENS NEXT?

SCOTT SUMMERS IS DEAD.

EITHER WE JUST WENT TO WAR WITH THE ENTIRE MUTANT POPULATION...

...OR THEY ARE GOING TO SEND US THE NICEST BOUQUET OF FLOWERS EVER SEEN.

I HONESTLY HAVE NO IDEA WHICH WAY THIS IS GOING TO GO.

TODAY.

HENRY, I ASKED YOU A QUESTION, WHERE IS SCOTT SUMMERS IN ALL OF THIS?

EMMA, LISTEN, SCOTT SUMMERS IS ACTIVELY TRYING TO *RECRUIT* THE NEW MUTANT.

OF COURSE HE IS.

THIS MUTANT WITH POWER OVER PHYSICS AND LIFE AND DEATH--

I CAN *DO* THE MATH.

A *CHILD* CAN DO THE MATH.

SCOTT IS MAKING HIS PLAY.

AND IN DOING SO, HE IS ONCE AGAIN GOING TO SPEAK FOR ALL OF US AND CROSS A LINE WITH THE HUMANS...

...OR THREATEN TO CROSS A LINE WHICH, AS WE ALL KNOW, IS EVEN *WORSE* IN SOME WAYS THAN *ACTUALLY* CROSSING THE LINE.

I'M--I'M GOING TO SAY SOMETHING HERE, AND IT MIGHT *SHOCK* SOME OF YOU...

...BUT I THINK IT IS *LONG PAST* THE TIME WHERE WE--

BEEP BEEP BEEP BEEP BEEP

WHAT *IS* THAT, HANK?

HOLD ON, STORM WAS ABOUT TO SAY SOMETHING.

OH, MY STARS...

...AND GARTERS...

XAVIER'S SCHOOL FOR GIFTED YOUNGSTERS.

YEARS AGO.

NO.

PLEASE. IT'S THE ONLY WAY I CAN GET YOU TO BELIEVE ME.

BUT IT'S *YOU* WHO TOOK THE CHANCE, PROFESSOR.

I'M SORRY.

BUT. IT IS.

I CAME HERE TO TELL YOU THAT THIS MUTANT THAT YOU'RE HIDING FROM EVERYONE...

...THIS MATTHEW MALLOY...

HE WAKES UP.

AS AN ADULT.

AND HE... HE CANNOT BE CONTROLLED.

THIS PLAN THAT YOU HAVE TO REPRESS HIS POWERS THROUGHOUT HIS CHILDHOOD DOESN'T WORK.

BECAUSE I AM NO LONGER *THERE* TO HELP HIM.

DEVIL'S TOWER.

NOW.

MATTHEW MALLOY IS--

I WILL *NOT* ALLOW YOU TO DO THIS, MISS BELL.

I WILL NOT ALLOW YOU TO COME HERE AND DEFY MY WISHES AND THE LEGACY OF THIS SCHOOL.

THIS IS *WRONG*.

MURDER IS WRONG.

I'M TELLING YOU, PEOPLE DIE.

THIS--

AT THE HANDS OF A MUTANT THAT *YOU*--

--THIS IS A CHANCE TOO LARGE FOR ANY ONE MUTANT TO TAKE RESPONSIBILITY FOR.

YOU NEED TO COME UP WITH ANOTHER PLAN.

ALL RIGHT BOYS, BAG 'EM AND TAG 'EM.

NO.

NO?

NO.

DIRECTOR HILL SAYS NO ONE IS TO TOUCH ANYTHING.

WHAT?

SHE CALLED FOR A FULL FORENSICS TEAM FOR ON-SITE.

ON-SITE?

WE KNOW THE CAUSE OF DEATH.

I *KNOW* WE KNOW.

DEATH BY MISSILE UP THE KEISTER.

I KNOW.

BUT SHE WANTS WHAT SHE WANTS.

I TELL YA, YOU PUT AN EYEPATCH ON HER AND THERE'S ABSOLUTELY *NO DIFFERENCE* BETWEEN HER AND THAT--

DUDE, COOL IT.

YOU KNOW THEY *RECORD* US.

I DID *NOT* KNOW THAT.

DID YOU JUST TRY TO KILL ME?

HOLY $%#&!

OH $%#&!

THE CRIME SCENE IS LIVE! I REPEAT, THE CRIME SCENE IS *STILL LIVE* AND THE SUSPECT IS--

FIRE!

YOU DON'T THINK THAT S.H.I.E.L.D. RECORDS EVERYTHING WE SAY IN OUR ARMOR?

UH, NO.

WELL THEN, YOU'RE THE DUMBEST S.H.I.E.L.D. AGENT SINCE THE GUY WHO--

EXCUSE ME.

FAKOOM FAKOOM FAKOOM

OW.

THING IS...

...I DIDN'T KNOW I COULD DO ANY OF THIS.

XAVIER'S SCHOOL FOR GIFTED YOUNGSTERS.

YEARS AGO.

NOT ONLY HAS THIS MATTHEW MALLOY ALREADY MURDERED, BUT SCOTT SUMMERS--YOUR PRIZE STUDENT, AND WHAT I'M SURE IS TO BE MY EX-TEACHER--IS USING HIM AS A *WEAPON* OR TRYING TO CONVINCE HIM TO *BE* A WEAPON IN THE CAUSE OF MUTANT FREEDOM.

THAT SOUNDS LIKE SOMETHING *MAGNETO* WOULD DO.

THIS IS SOMETHING THAT MAGNETO TRIED TO *STOP*.

IT'S MY FAULT.

WHAT IS?

CYCLOPS.

HE HAD A NERVOUS BREAKDOWN AFTER CHARLES XAVIER'S DEATH AND I DIDN'T DO ANYTHING TO HELP HIM.

BECAUSE... BECAUSE I WAS *ANGRY* WITH HIM.

I STILL AM.

I DIDN'T DO ANYTHING TO STOP HIM FROM PUTTING HIMSELF, OR US, IN HARM'S WAY.

AND NOW?

NOW IT IS *TOO LATE.*

LEAVE ME BE!

THIS IS ALL VERY UPSETTING.

OBVIOUSLY.

I DON'T KNOW WHAT YOU SHOULD DO, BUT YOU HAVE TO DO *SOMETHING.*

I WILL NOT KILL A CHILD.

EVEN IF THAT CHILD KILLS AND CANNOT BE STOPPED?

I AM SO OFFENDED BY YOU BEING HERE.

YOU'VE RUINED MY LIFE.

WE HAVE AN EXPRESSION WHERE I'M FROM ABOUT NOT KILLING THE MESSENGER.

I COULD WIPE YOUR MIND AND PSYCHICALLY COMMAND YOU TO JUST WALK AWAY.

AND THAT WOULD BE THE END OF YOU.

OH, THIS IS THE OTHER CHARLES XAVIER I'VE HEARD ABOUT.

THE ONE THAT TEACHES ONE THING BUT SAYS *"THE HELL WITH IT"* WHEN IT'S INCONVENIENT.

I...I DIDN'T MEAN THAT.

SHE WAS GOING TO KILL ME.

I...I CAN'T BRING HER BACK.

WHO WAS SHE?

THE NEW XAVIER SCHOOL.

TODAY.

HAS ANYONE SEEN EVA?

I DON'T LIKE THIS. SOMETHING IS GOING ON.

YEAH, UH *DOY,* HIJACK.

NO. I MEAN SOMETHING WE DON'T EVEN KNOW ABOUT.

THEY HAVE US LOCKED DOWN HERE...THE ORIGINAL X-MEN ARE NOWHERE TO BE FOUND... THEY TOOK THE PLANE...

...OUR PROFESSOR WHO TELEPORTS HAS TELEPORTED EVERYONE ELSE OUT OF HERE EXCEPT FOR US.

I THINK MAGNETO LEFT, TOO.

THAT'S IT!

WHAT'S IT?

I'M TAKING THE PLANE, CHRISTOPHER, AND I'M--

THEY TOOK THE PLANE.

I'M A MUTANT THAT CAN *CONTROL MACHINES.*

THERE MUST BE SOMETHING AROUND HERE I CAN HIJACK.

LADIES?

UM?

I THINK THEY ARE BUSY IN THEIR HIVE-MIND THING AND NOT TALKING TO US?

I DON'T BLAME THEM.

AAANGGHH!

GYYAAAGGHH!

NOOO!

OH, MY GOD!

OH, MY GOD!

WH-WHAT HAPPENED?

MISS FROST...

WE HAD HER IN OUR HIVEMIND. JUST IN CASE.

JUST TO-- JUST TO KEEP TABS ON--ON--ON--

WHAT HAPPENED TO HER?

SHE-- --SHE'S GONE.

OH NOOOO...

HOW?

WHO DID IT?

THE-- THE NEW MUTANT.

THAT'S IT!

WE DO SOMETHING. WE GET IN THE GAME.

WHAT? WHAT DO WE DO?

I'M IN.

BUT WE-- WE HAVE NOTHING.

I, UH, I HAVE SOMETHING.

UM...

IS THAT...?

WHAT HAVE YOU DONE?

TO ME, MY X-MEN.

UNCANNY X-MEN #30 WELCOME HOME VARIANT
BY SALVADOR LARROCA & ISRAEL SILVA

UH...

WHAT *NEEDED* TO BE DONE, DAVID!

X-MEN. THERE'S NO REASON TO PANIC.

OH MY GOD!

IT'S HIM, CELESTE! IT'S REALLY HIM!

HOLY $#%&, CHARLES XAVIER!

...IS THIS REAL?

OH

MY

GOD!

EVA, WHAT DID YOU *DO*?

HE OOKS SO OUNG.

I'M MORE FOCUSED ON THE FACT THAT HE LOOKS *ALIVE*.

EVA?
EVA, BEFORE I PSYCHICALLY FORCE YOU TO PUT HIM BACK WHERE YOU FOUND HIM, WIPE HIS BRAIN, LOBOTOMIZE YOU AND THEN LOBOTOMIZE *MYSELF* TO FORGET THIS EVER HAPPENED...

...ANSWER ME...

...WHYYYYY?!

BECAUSE THERE'S AN OUT OF CONTROL MUTANT RUINING ANY HOPE WE HAVE FOR THIS WORLD.

YOU HEARD MAGNETO, WE'RE IN OVER--

THIS WAS *NOT* YOUR CALL!

I'M A PERSON LIVING ON THE PLANET EARTH.

IT'S MY CALL AS MUCH AS ANYONE'S.

STUDENTS. LET'S TAKE A MOMENT TO COLLECT OURSELVES.

WHAT IS DONE IS DONE.

LET'S FIND A *SOLUTION* TO THIS SURREAL EXPERIENCE AND--

WHOOOP WHOOOPP

IT IS IMPORTANT TO ME AND TO OUR PEOPLE THAT YOU SURVIVE THIS DAY.

I PROMISE YOU I HAVE ABSOLUTELY NO HESITATION SACRIFICING MY LIFE SO THAT YOU CAN LIVE YOURS...

...BUT IF YOU GO INTO BATTLE NOW, HALF-COCKED, TO AVENGE ME OR THE OTHER TEACHERS OF THE SCHOOL WITHOUT PROPER TRAINING...YOU WILL BE BETRAYING MY FINAL WISHES.

WE STILL LIVE IN A DANGEROUS WORLD THAT MAY NOT BE READY FOR OUR KIND...

...BUT I WANT YOU TO LIVE LONG ENOUGH SO THAT YOU OR YOUR CHILDREN CAN SEE THE DAY OUR DREAM COMES TRUE.

THIS PLANE IS PROGRAMMED TO TAKE YOU WHERE THE LEADERS OF OUR COMMUNITY AND MY FORMER TEAMMATES WILL TAKE YOU IN.

THERE IS NOWHERE SAFER ON EARTH FOR YOU NOW THAN THE JEAN GREY SCHOOL.

I HOPE.

HELP US.

WHERE IS THIS "JEAN GREY SCHOOL"?

AUSTIN, TEXAS.
YEARS AGO...

THIS WAS...

WHERE MATTHEW WAS BORN AND RAISED.

WHERE I FIRST MET HIM.

THIS IS THE DAY I FIRST MET HIM.

I JUST WANTED TO SEE...

HOW WORRIED ARE WE ABOUT THE BUTTERFLY EFFECT?

MISS BELL, PLEASE...

"OKAY.

"I, CHARLES FRANCIS XAVIER, OF THE TOWN OF SALEM..."

THERE HAS TO BE A WAY TO TOSS THIS WILL IN THE GARBAGE!

NOT LEGALLY.

WELL, CALL MATT MURDOCK.

WHY?

BECAUSE HE'S THE ONLY OTHER LAWYER I'VE EVER HEARD OF!

I'M SIGNING IT OVER TO ORORO.

ALL OF IT. EVERYTHING. IF XAVIER WERE ALIVE I KNOW, WE ALL KNOW, THAT'S WHAT HE WOULD HAVE WANTED.

DO WE MAYBE WANT TO TALK THIS OVER FIRST?

I WAS WONDERING IF, IN RETURN, YOU MIGHT DO ME A FAVOR.

HERE WE GO...

WE HAVE STUDENTS AT OUR TRAINING SCHOOL. GOOD MUTANTS. WOULD YOU DO ME THE COURTESY OF TAKING THEM IN?

EXCUSE ME?

UM...

WHAT ARE *YOU* GOING TO DO?

I DON'T KNOW.

I KNOW SOME OF YOU HATE ME, BUT I LOVE EVERYONE IN THIS ROOM.

I REALLY DO.

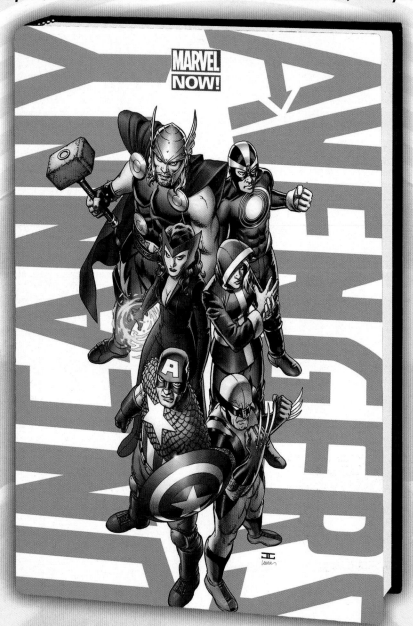

UNCANNY AVENGERS VOL. 1: THE RED SHADOW
WRITTEN BY RICK REMENDER • ART BY JOHN CASSADAY
978-0-7851-6603-0 • DEC130776

© 2013 MARVEL